REPTILES

GIANT TORTOISES

BY MEGAN GENDELL

WWW.APEXEDITIONS.COM

Copyright © 2024 by Apex Editions, Mendota Heights, MN 55120. All rights reserved. No part of this book may be reproduced or utilized in any form or by any means without written permission from the publisher.

Apex is distributed by North Star Editions:
sales@northstareditions.com | 888-417-0195

Produced for Apex by Red Line Editorial.

Photographs ©: iStockphoto, cover, 8–9, 16–17, 26; Shutterstock Images, 1, 4–5, 6–7, 10–11, 12–13, 15, 18, 19, 20, 22–23, 24–25, 27, 29; Lieutenant Elizabeth Crapo/NOAA Corps/NOAA, 14

Library of Congress Control Number: 2022920181

ISBN
978-1-63738-544-9 (hardcover)
978-1-63738-598-2 (paperback)
978-1-63738-703-0 (ebook pdf)
978-1-63738-652-1 (hosted ebook)

Printed in the United States of America
Mankato, MN
082023

NOTE TO PARENTS AND EDUCATORS
Apex books are designed to build literacy skills in striving readers. Exciting, high-interest content attracts and holds readers' attention. The text is carefully leveled to allow students to achieve success quickly. Additional features, such as bolded glossary words for difficult terms, help build comprehension.

TABLE OF CONTENTS

CHAPTER 1
FACE-TO-FACE 4

CHAPTER 2
BIG AND STRONG 10

CHAPTER 3
EATING TIME 16

CHAPTER 4
LIFE IN THE WILD 22

COMPREHENSION QUESTIONS • 28
GLOSSARY • 30
TO LEARN MORE • 31
ABOUT THE AUTHOR • 31
INDEX • 32

CHAPTER 1

FACE-TO-FACE

A giant tortoise walks slowly. He follows a narrow dirt path in the woods. A bigger tortoise comes toward him. The path is too small for both to fit. One will have to move.

A tortoise's front feet are turned inward. So, its body wobbles a little with each step.

The two tortoises reach each other. Each lifts its head. The first tortoise is smaller. But it raises its head higher.

The fronts of some shells give tortoises extra space to lift their heads.

HEADS UP

Male giant tortoises lift their heads to show **dominance**. The tortoise with the highest head wins. That tortoise gets his choice of food or **mate**.

The bigger tortoise lowers his head. He turns and moves out of the way. The first tortoise continues down the path.

FAST FACT

Sometimes tortoises open their mouths as a **threat**. But they rarely bite.

Giant tortoises spend most of their time on land.

CHAPTER 2

Big and Strong

Giant tortoises are **reptiles**. They have thick, strong legs. Their skin is tough and covered in scales. Each tortoise has a large shell on its back.

10

Giant tortoises and their shells are usually gray or brown.

There are two main kinds of giant tortoises. Aldabra tortoises live on Aldabra Island. This **tropical** island is southeast of Africa.

Aldabra tortoises can be 4 feet (1.2 m) long.

FAST FACT

The heaviest Aldabra tortoise weighed 672 pounds (305 kg).

The Galápagos Islands are home to many animal species. Some live nowhere else in the world.

Galápagos tortoises live on the Galápagos Islands. Those rocky islands are east of South America. Galápagos tortoises are the biggest. They can weigh more than 900 pounds (408 kg).

SLOWPOKES

Tortoises move very slowly. It takes a Galápagos tortoise more than six hours to walk 1 mile (1.6 km). The average human takes 21 minutes to go that far.

Galápagos tortoises can be 6 feet (1.8 m) long.

CHAPTER 3

Eating Time

Giant tortoises are mainly **herbivores**. They eat grass, fruit, and leaves. Galápagos tortoises also eat cactus pads.

The prickly pear cactus grows all around the Galápagos Islands.

A tortoise's sharp mouth can bite through tough or prickly plants.

Tortoises have no teeth. But the edges of their mouths are sharp. They tear off plants to eat. Giant tortoises don't need to eat or drink very often. Many live in dry places.

FAST FACT

Some giant tortoises can go a year without food or water.

Giant tortoises often eat plants that grow along the ground. In dry places, they may reach higher to find food.

A giant tortoise's shell can protect it from most **predators**. The tortoise pulls its head and legs inside. But some animals eat baby tortoises.

SAVING TORTOISES

In the past, giant tortoises almost went **extinct**. Humans hunted many of them. Others were killed by animals that people brought to the islands. Today, people work hard to keep giant tortoises safe.

◀ A tortoise's shell has two main parts. They go above and below its body.

CHAPTER 4

LIFE IN THE WILD

Giant tortoises begin to mate when they're about 25 years old. After mating, female tortoises dig nests. They lay eggs inside.

Male giant tortoises are usually larger than females.

Each egg is the size of a tennis ball. The female covers her eggs to hide them. Then she leaves the nest.

MAKING MUD

After laying eggs, a tortoise may pee around her nest. Mud forms. The tortoise covers her eggs with this mud. She presses it down with her belly.

Giant tortoises sometimes take mud baths to stay cool.

Baby tortoises hatch about four months later. The **hatchlings** often stay in the nest for a few weeks. After that, they live on their own.

Baby giant tortoises dig to the surface after hatching.

Giant tortoises continue growing throughout their lives.

FAST FACT
Giant tortoises can live for more than 100 years in the wild.

COMPREHENSION QUESTIONS

Write your answers on a separate piece of paper.

1. Write a few sentences describing the life cycle of a giant tortoise.

2. Some giant tortoises live in dry places. Would you rather live somewhere wet or dry? Why?

3. What is a food that giant tortoises eat?
    - A. grass
    - B. birds
    - C. snakes

4. Why would a female tortoise cover and hide her eggs?
    - A. so the eggs will not hatch
    - B. so a male tortoise will not find them
    - C. so predators will not find and eat them

5. What does **tough** mean in this book?

*Their skin is **tough** and covered in scales.*

    A. thick and strong
    B. weak and soft
    C. hard to read

6. What does **protect** mean in this book?

*A giant tortoise's shell can **protect** it from most predators. The tortoise pulls its head and legs inside.*

    A. cause harm
    B. break something
    C. keep safe

Answer key on page 32.

GLOSSARY

dominance
Having more power or getting first choice of resources such as food, water, or mates.

extinct
No longer living on Earth.

hatchlings
Young animals that have recently hatched from eggs.

herbivores
Animals that eat mostly plants.

mate
One of a pair of animals that come together to have babies.

predators
Animals that hunt and eat other animals.

reptiles
Cold-blooded animals that have scales.

threat
A way of scaring others so they will do something.

tropical
Having weather that is often warm and wet.

BOOKS

Jackson, Tom. *World's Biggest Reptiles*. Minneapolis: Lerner Publications, 2019.

Jaycox, Jaclyn. *Giant Tortoises*. North Mankato, MN: Capstone Press, 2021.

Ringstad, Arnold. *Totally Amazing Facts about Reptiles*. North Mankato, MN: Capstone Press, 2018.

ONLINE RESOURCES

Visit **www.apexeditions.com** to find links and resources related to this title.

ABOUT THE AUTHOR

Megan Gendell is a writer and editor. She likes to take long walks and watch birds fly above mountaintops.

INDEX

A
Aldabra Island, 12
Aldabra tortoises, 12–13

C
cactus, 16

E
eggs, 22, 24–25
extinction, 21

G
Galápagos Islands, 14
Galápagos tortoises, 14–15, 16

H
hatching, 26
herbivores, 16

M
mating, 7, 22
mouth, 8, 18

P
predators, 21

R
reptiles, 10

S
shell, 10, 21
skin, 10

T
threat, 8
tropical, 12

ANSWER KEY:
1. Answers will vary; 2. Answers will vary; 3. A; 4. C; 5. A; 6. C